YOUR DOG
IN 7 DAYS

HOW TO HOUSEBREAK YOUR DOG IN 7 DAYS

Shirlee Kalstone

Illustrations by Pamela Powers

Bantam Books

HOW TO HOUSEBREAK YOUR DOG IN 7 DAYS
A Bantam Book / August 2004

Published by Bantam Dell
A Division of Random House, Inc.
New York, New York

Cover design by Beverly Leung

Book design by Virginia Norey

Library of Congress Cataloging-in-Publication Data
Kalstone, Shirlee.
How to housebreak your dog in 7 days / Shirlee Kalstone ;
illustrations by Pamela Powers.—Rev.
p. cm.
Includes bibliographical references (p.).
ISBN 0-553-38289-6
1. Dogs—Training. I. Title.

SF431.K35 2004
636.7'0887—dc22   2003063648

Manufactured in the United States of America
Published simultaneously in Canada

OPM   20 19 18 17 16 15 14 13 12 11

CONTENTS

HOW TO HOUSEBREAK YOUR DOG IN 7 DAYS

INTRODUCTION

Owning a dog is one of life's great joys. But dog ownership is a long-term commitment, since healthy dogs can live fifteen years or more. It's a lot more pleasant to share your existence with a dog that is well trained and not a nuisance. Training isn't just for the sake of others, either; no one, no matter how much that person loves his or her pet, wants to live with a disobedient animal that leaves "calling cards" all over the rugs and floors. Every dog *should* be housebroken, and there are few exceptions to the rule that every dog *can* be housebroken.

My first introduction to dogs was in early childhood. My mother was a Cocker Spaniel fancier, and I grew up surrounded by the most enchanting jet-black and taffy-colored creatures. The first dog of my very own, Buzzy, shared my toys and slept in my bed. Is it any wonder that when I became old enough to choose a career, my life (pardon the pun) went to the dogs? My experience over forty years as a breeder and exhibitor of Poodles, Whippets, English Setters, Cocker Spaniels, Weimaraners, and Burmese and British Shorthair cats, and as a trainer, groomer, humane worker, and a teacher, lecturer, and writer on the subject of dogs and cats, has brought me into contact with pet people throughout the world. I've seen almost every kind of canine problem behavior.

I wrote this book to make housebreaking less aggravating for pet owners. In training my own puppies, I learned years ago that dogs can be housebroken in a short time by following a simple formula:

feed them regular and nutritious meals, put them on a strict outdoor-walking or indoor-paper schedule, confine them at night and at specific times during the day until they can be trusted to have the run of the house, and give them plenty of praise. It sounds elementary, yet during my work at animal shelters I discovered that more dogs lose their homes because they are not housetrained than for any other reason.

William Campbell, a leading authority on canine behavior, writes in *Behavior Problems in Dogs*, "Puppies first become fastidious and avoid 'messing' in their litter homes at about five weeks of age. If we can use this tendency in the pup's new human home, the housebreaking chore can be accomplished within days, rather than the more commonly required weeks or months."

Training of any kind is basically communication between owner and dog, and I'm convinced that most housebreaking failures usually are the owner's fault. Barbara Woodhouse, the famous British dog trainer, once said there are no bad dogs, only inexperienced owners—and she's right. When a healthy dog cannot be housebroken within a week, give or take a few days, it's probably due to the owner's procrastination or inconsistency. Either the owner hasn't the foggiest notion of how to proceed, or is too lazy to follow a simple training program even for seven days, and the undisciplined dog develops bad habits that are nearly impossible to break. The owner often gets frustrated and punishes the dog, causing physical or emotional damage. Rubbing a dog's nose in any mess he makes, yelling, beating, and other harsh reprimands do nothing to further housebreaking and, in fact, only help to suppress a dog's temperament. Modern trainers hardly ever resort to force, because they know they can accomplish more with positive reinforcement—that is, praising good behavior.

The key to successful housebreaking is to begin the day your dog joins your family. If yours is a baby puppy, keep in mind that he is too young to control bladder and bowel movements for very long. Until he's ready for formal housebreaking, though, you can at least begin to lay the groundwork for it. (See "The Very Young Puppy," page 11.) Ultimately, it is your responsibility to teach the dog to urinate and defecate outdoors in the yard or in the street, or indoors on newspapers, or at any other place of *your*—not the dog's—choosing.

Please read this book from beginning to end before undertaking any of the procedures. It sets forth a specific method of training rather than random suggestions. If you read the book carefully, follow the simple formula, use common sense to prevent accidents from happening, have patience, and praise your dog's positive behavior, you can look forward to a housebroken dog that is a joy to live with. *It's very easy. There are no gimmicks. It's a strict but not a hard-hearted system.*

Your dog will willingly and eagerly do virtually anything to please you if you just show him what you want. You *can* housebreak your dog in a week once you learn the system and understand the concept behind it. And isn't it worth spending just seven days to derive years of pleasure from a well-mannered dog?

The training program has been successful for me and for my clients. With a little determination, it will work for you. Happy housebreaking!

THE PSYCHOLOGY OF TRAINING: DOGS ARE PACK ANIMALS THAT RESPOND TO A STRONG LEADER

The 7-day housebreaking formula is based in part on your dog's inherited behavioral instincts. Dogs are social creatures that readily adapt to dominance-subordination relationships. They prefer to live in groups, or "packs," rather than alone. A bond of attachment formed among the pack members keeps the group together. But the bond by itself is not enough to maintain order in the group. There is also a leader and a chain of command.

Canine pack relationships are based on a dominance hierarchy, or a descending "pecking" order. There is always one dog in each group that becomes the pack leader. The leader will dominate, establish organization, discipline the rest, and maintain group order. Other pack members rarely challenge the leader. Next in rank is the second-in-command. He or she is controlled only by the leader but, in turn, dominates all the pack members below in rank. Every member of the pack has a position in the hierarchy, and once these positions are established, each dog knows precisely which members are above him in rank and which are beneath him, and what his role is.

In all the pack's activities in the wild, the leader firmly shows the other members that he is boss. He will take the initiative in play, and he will become the first to mate. He will eat first after a hunt, but once he has his fill, the other dogs take turns at eating in hierarchical order. The leader will defend his possessions—his living quarters, food, and mate—at all costs. The chain of command will change, of course, over the years. Young adults, always on the alert for weaknesses in others, may try to defy more dominant older dogs, and rise to a higher position in the hierarchy if they are victorious. Younger and stronger dogs eventually assume authority in this manner as the dominant animals grow older and less healthy and vigorous. Dogs *always* inherit these pack tendencies, whether they are wild or domesticated.

The same pack behavior patterns govern a dog's relationships with humans. Once a dog enters a new home, you can simply interchange the word "pack" with the term "family." All the members of the household are part of the pack in the dog's eyes. It is extremely important, therefore, that your dog learn his position in the family hierarchy immediately to ensure a well-trained and dependable pet.

A dominant-subordinate relationship is imperative in all types of dog training, especially housebreaking. As soon as you get the new puppy or adult dog, you or some other member of your family must assume the role of pack leader—with the dog as subordinate—by establishing the rules and enforcing them fairly. You must maintain a firm but loving attitude, and once you have assumed the role of leader, you must *always* play it. If no family member takes the controlling position, the dog will dominate, and you will end up with a spoiled beast that will be difficult, if not impossible, to housetrain. A dog in a new home will test you and other family members until he finds his place. Unless you understand that this initial testing is a way of determining how far he can go, the animal will develop behavior problems. And the problems of an undisciplined dog only get worse as he matures.

THE SECRET OF
SUCCESSFUL HOUSEBREAKING

You have learned that dogs are easy animals to train because they are pack animals with strong tendencies to follow a leader. The secret of successful and rapid housebreaking is to understand that dogs are also den dwellers in their natural state. In the wild, dogs hunt for food, mate, socialize with fellow pack members, and relieve themselves *outside* their dens. But they always return to their dens, snug and sheltered nests where they feel comfortable and secure, to sleep. Den dwellers will never soil their nests, and this is the prime reason that dogs can be housetrained so easily.

Teaching a normal healthy puppy, or even an adult dog, to eliminate in a particular spot is a lot easier than you might imagine, because dogs are naturally clean from birth. For the first three weeks of life, the reflexes and behavioral responses of newborn puppies are directed totally to their mother. They can't see or hear until the fourteenth day, but they can crawl and suckle. Mother feeds the puppies, keeps them warm in her nest, cleans them, and controls their elimination. After feeding, she stimulates excretion by licking each puppy's genitals and anus. Puppies form their first social bonds with their mother and, like human babies, they respond to her affection and attention.

Between the ages of four and five weeks, when the puppies attain their sensory and motor abilities, their mother gives them less intensive care, and they become independent enough to toddle in and out of their nest. Social bonds among brothers and sisters begin to develop. The puppies become curious and begin to explore and play together in a lively manner. They also start to bite and fight among themselves as each puppy tries to prevail over the others. In this manner, the puppies begin to ascertain the strengths and weaknesses of their littermates and take the first steps to determine dominance and submission.

Puppies first become fastidious at about five weeks of age. They can defecate and urinate now without stimulation, and, from this moment, they start going to a particular spot away from their nest to relieve themselves. If a puppy's owner takes advantage of this natural instinct, housebreaking *can* be accomplished in days, instead of weeks or months.

You must also become familiar with your dog's natural excretory instincts. Dogs, like people, usually want to urinate and sometimes to defecate when they wake up. Most dogs, though, tend to have bowel movements about 20 to 30 minutes after eating. It's not hard to determine when your dog should go out, or be placed on his paper, once you understand these basic rhythms.

WHEN IS MY DOG
READY TO BE HOUSEBROKEN?

Behaviorists have determined that the basis of dog training is a bond of attachment or respect formed between animals and human beings. They say the bond is best established when a puppy is between six and eight weeks of age because the early formation of a strong social bond makes a dog more eager to please his master and more attentive during training.

Most animal behaviorists recommend separating a puppy from his mother and littermates at about seven to eight weeks of age and placing him in a home with *loving* people. The puppy will be more inclined to become a member of the family pack at this age; he will become more attached to his owner and be more trainable. If you obtained your puppy from a reliable breeder, the puppy's socialization should have been carefully orchestrated. The puppy will have had social periods with his mother and brothers and sisters, and he will also have received plenty of handling and cuddling by human beings, giving you a well-adjusted animal that will adapt easily to your lifestyle.

A puppy's infancy is very short compared to a human baby's: three to four canine months are roughly equal to three to four human years. While there is no magic age for a child to start using the potty or toilet—some toddlers begin around the age of two, while others aren't ready until they're older—generally the average child is successfully toilet trained by four years old. Correspondingly, the average puppy should be housebroken by four months of age. Please bear in mind the word "average." Just as every child is different, every puppy is different. If your puppy isn't housebroken by four months of age, take your time. Don't press him too hard. Stick to the program. Even though housebreaking may take a little longer, at least the puppy will begin to comprehend the principles of it all.

THE VERY YOUNG PUPPY

You can't expect too much in the way of housebreaking before your puppy is sixteen weeks old, because he does not yet have full sphincter muscle control. *Puppies simply cannot hold bladder and bowel movements for long periods at this age.* The interval between the urge and the act of urination or defecation is very short. Unless you immediately notice the distinctive movements a puppy makes when he's looking to relieve himself, like sniffing the floor to search for a good toilet spot or going around in circles, he'll probably soil your floor. Your principal duty at this time is keep the puppy from having the run of the house to urinate and defecate on the carpets and floors. However, at this stage of a puppy's life, virtually every action is a learning experience, so it's an ideal time to begin informal housebreaking preliminaries to establish good habits.

Now is the perfect opportunity to start taking advantage of the puppy's inherent den-dwelling instincts—which compel him to keep his sleeping and eating areas clean and to move away to urinate or defecate. It's impossible to watch the youngster all the time, of course, so the temporary solution (until he reaches sixteen weeks of age) is to confine him to a "nursery" area completely covered with newspapers in a room such as the kitchen, where there is a washable floor. Don't give him the run of the entire kitchen if it's very large; restrict him by blocking off a small area within the room or confine him to a large, portable puppy-exercise pen. The size of the restricted area will vary with the size of the puppy, but it should be no larger than 3 by 5 feet. Make him a comfortable bed at one end (or place a wire crate there with the door open)* where he can sit, lie down, turn around, and see everything that's going on, but with room for him to go to the other end to eliminate. Just make sure his entire area is covered with newspaper so that he can't eliminate on the bare floor.

Start immediately to let him know what's expected. Housebreaking and paper-training are two different practices. (See pages 16 and 30.) If your ultimate goal is paper-training, then each time the puppy walks away from his sleeping area and uses his paper, tell him he is the most wonderful and clever dog in the world, and by the time he's sixteen weeks old, he will be almost paper-trained already. If you want him to eventually urinate and defecate outside, then *don't* deliberately praise him when he uses the papers. Simply pick up the soiled papers as quickly as possible and put down fresh ones. Praise, in this situation, sends him a message that it's okay to mess in the house. You don't want to confuse the puppy about where to relieve himself if he's going to go outdoors in a short time. Once he's fully vaccinated against distemper and other infectious and contagious canine diseases, you can begin leash training (see page 31),

---

*When the puppy's approximately sixteen weeks old, you can begin the more formal housebreaking schedule that is the subject of this book, in which confinement, most likely in a wire crate, plays an important role. Confinement in a crate, unless you are away from home for long periods during the day, is the best way to housebreak dogs of any age. (See "Confining Your Dog to a 'Den'" on page 23.) Here's a suggestion: if you do plan to use a crate for your puppy's confinement, consider buying it now. Place the crate at one end of his temporary "den," **keep the door open,** and let him use it as a bed. At this impressionable age, you don't want the puppy to feel like he's shut up in prison, but, by letting him go into and out of the crate at will, you do want him to start associating it as a place of refuge. By the time he's sixteen weeks old, he'll be well on the way to being crate-trained.

and take him outside on an informal basis until he gains more muscle control and is ready for real housebreaking.

Keep your puppy clean and change his papers frequently. Don't be too strict with him—puppies go through a fear-imprint stage between eight and twelve weeks of age, and how you treat the puppy now will affect his behavior forever. Harsh punishment should be avoided. Let him meet new people, children, and other animals, let him be gently handled and petted, but do not force him into any situation that frightens him. Do not let anyone deliberately scare or hurt the puppy. Even a seemingly insignificant episode can destroy the bond you want to establish, and intimidate the puppy for months. An experience that produces trembling at this stage might affect your puppy for life.

Most people postpone even gentle early training because they think puppies can't learn much. "Not true," says Dr. Michael Fox, one of the world's best-known animal behaviorists. "A young puppy is a highly responsible creature with an incredible capacity to explore its environment and learn new things every day. There is a critical period between eight and twelve weeks of age when a puppy's inclination to explore and acquire knowledge is set. If experiences and simple training or handling are denied or limited during this early period, the puppy will have a lower IQ as an adult dog." You can read more about the fascinating subjects of canine socialization and behavior in Dr. Fox's classic *Understanding Your Dog: Everything You Want to Know About Your Dog but Haven't Been Able to Ask Him* (St. Martin's Press, 1992).

WHAT ABOUT OLDER DOGS?

Let's suppose that (a) you already have a dog that is an undisciplined brat, (b) you are adopting an older dog that has never been housetrained, or (c) you are bringing one home from a shelter and he has regressed because he has not been able to eliminate outdoors. This book isn't for you, right?

Wrong! No dog is too bad or too old to learn. Consider this corrective training and begin the 7-day program at once. Housebreaking an adult dog is no different than housebreaking a puppy—it will only take longer because naughty dogs, untrained dogs, or regressive dogs have been doing things their own way for so long that their bad habits have become deeply rooted. The older the untrained dog, the longer it will take for his natural instincts to reappear. You'll have to work harder to bring them forth, but it can be done, though it may indeed take a little longer than seven days. Stick with the program. Watch the dog closely, and when you can't, confine him to a den. Feed him on a fixed schedule, once or twice a day, to help regulate his urination and defecation. Once your dog is trained, you'll have to take him out only three or four times a day, and your life will be easier. And don't forget that older dogs have better control of their bladder and bowels; once housetrained, they can control the urge to eliminate for longer time periods than puppies can.

Adult dogs that are already housebroken sometimes regress and begin urinating and defecating in the house. Have the dog examined by a veterinarian to rule out any health problems. If illness is not the cause, the accidents are probably hormonal or behavioral in nature. Read more about these under "Housebreaking and Paper-Training Problems" (page 64).

YOUR CHOICE:
HOUSEBREAKING, PAPER-TRAINING,
OR LITTER PAN TRAINING

The best time to start training your dog is the day he comes into your home. The first few days in a new environment are vital for teaching good habits. The puppy's health plays an important role in successful housebreaking. He should be examined by a veterinarian within forty-eight hours after he enters your home, in order to determine that he is in good health and not suffering from urinary tract problems or other internal parasites that could interfere with the training program. Read more about this in the "Health Problems" section of "Housebreaking and Paper-Training Problems" (page 64).

The 7-day formula is recommended for puppies sixteen weeks of age or older. However, remember that you can start "pre-training" puppies that are very young (under four months) by shaping their behavior until they are old enough for formal housetraining to begin. (See "The Very Young Puppy," page 11).

You must decide what form of training best fits your lifestyle: housebreaking, paper-training, or litter pan training. Once the decision is made, you and every member of your family must follow the formula step-by-step. Housebreaking and paper-training a dog are two different practices, and each has its own special requirements. Housebreaking means that a dog is trained to urinate and defecate outdoors and that he is *never* allowed to soil indoors. Paper-training means that the dog is trained to urinate and defecate on several layers of newspapers that are placed at all times in the same location inside your house. Paper-training or litter pan training is useful if you own a small dog and live in an apartment, if you are handicapped or elderly and it is not easy to walk the dog, and for geriatric dogs whose medical conditions cause increased urination. *Paper-training is not the first step toward outdoor training.* Although paper-training may serve as a temporary substitute for very young puppies that cannot go out, paper-training is primarily for dogs that will always relieve themselves indoors, and it should be avoided if you ultimately expect your dog to urinate and defecate outside. The same training method and schedules can be used for housebreaking, paper-training, or litter pan training.

THE 7-DAY FORMULA

The 7-day formula for successful housebreaking, paper-training, or litter pan training is based on six principles:

1. Establishing regular eating habits.

2. Confining your dog to a "den" where he won't want to relieve himself.

3. Following a strict outdoor walking schedule, indoor-papering, or litter pan schedule.

4. Giving the dog plenty of praise.

5. Using immediate and consistent good discipline and corrective training.

6. Getting rid of odors promptly.

ESTABLISHING
REGULAR EATING HABITS

Regularity and consistency are essential parts of any training program, especially with a matter as crucial as housebreaking. Establishing sensible eating habits from day one, therefore, is the first step in the 7-day formula. Regular habits encourage a steady appetite and help to speed up housebreaking by regulating a dog's digestive processes. What goes in on schedule comes out on schedule—it's very elementary.

Most veterinarians, dog trainers, and breeders agree that dogs do best on a well-balanced commercial dog food. A well-balanced diet is one that contains the correct proportions of the essential nutrients—protein, carbohydrates, fat, vitamins, and minerals—in sufficient quantity and quality to maintain optimum health through each stage of a dog's life cycle. Today, a growing array of general-purpose foods—dry, canned, and semi-moist—and special-purpose foods nourish all breeds of dogs. General-purpose foods are formulated to meet the life-cycle needs of all breeds. Special-purpose foods are designed to meet the nutritional requirements of special classes of dogs, such as puppies, dogs under stress, pregnant and nursing bitches, fat dogs, old dogs, and dogs with kidney or intestinal problems, to name a few. The commercial foods and the prescription diets available on your supermarket or pet store shelves, or from veterinarians, are the results of years of conscientious research, and they save you the time and trouble of having to concoct nutritional meals on your own.

The more a dog eats and drinks, the more often he will relieve himself. It is important, therefore, to feed your dog the right amount of food to start with. The amount of food required is influenced by a dog's breed, size, age, temperament, environment, climate, and activity level. The quantity will vary, therefore, even among dogs of the same breed. Most dog food companies list the caloric content of a food and the recommended feeding amounts by weight on their packages. These may be used as guidelines. Start with the package recommendations and adjust your dog's intake if he seems hungry all the time or if he's getting a little paunchy. Talk to your veterinarian if you are confused. He or she will recommend the diet and feeding program that will best meet your dog's individual needs.

The Regular Routine

Once you decide on a food, it's not necessary to keep changing menus. Dogs are content to eat the same thing day after day. They also like to eat in the same location, at the same time, and from the same clean dish every day. It may sound boring to you, but it's reassuring to them. Set up a feeding schedule that you can adhere to. Put the feeding dish down, keep distractions at a minimum, give your dog about 15 to 20 minutes to eat, then remove the uneaten portion. This will teach your dog to eat promptly and not to linger over his food. More importantly, it will expedite housetraining, since most dogs usually relieve themselves shortly after eating and drinking. With young puppies, there's a very short interval between feeding and elimination. It's important to follow mealtimes with lessons in paper-training or housebreaking without delay. As a dog matures, he can hold things longer and will need to relieve himself less often. *Do not let your dog have unlimited access to food during the training period.* This will only cause constant elimination. And until good eating habits are established, avoid offering treats, table scraps, or home-cooked meals. Frequent dietary changes will only encourage your dog to become a finicky eater and cause stomach upsets or diarrhea, which will slow down the training schedule. You may wish to follow this feeding schedule:

RECOMMENDED FEEDING SCHEDULE

Age of Dog	Number of Feedings	Time of Day
Weaning to 3 months	4	Morning, noon, late afternoon, and evening*
3 to 6 months	3	Morning, afternoon, and evening*
6 to 12 months	2	Morning and late afternoon or early evening
1 year and over	1	Morning. Large and giant-sized breeds may require 2 meals per day. Feed second meal in late afternoon or early evening.

*Give food and water in the evening at least one hour before bedtime to allow the puppy time to digest his food, and to urinate and defecate, before going to sleep.

Water

Water is an important element in your dog's diet. It is the primary transporter of nutrients through the body, and it is linked with digestion as well as nearly every other body process. Water maintains a dog's normal body temperature and is essential for carrying waste material out of the body.

During the housebreaking period, you should offer your dog a drink of water at specific times indicated on the schedule you choose. (Schedules begin on page 51.) Let him drink as much as he wants, but pick up his bowl after 10 minutes. *Your dog's water will be limited only for the duration of the training period.* Once he is housebroken, he should have an unlimited supply of fresh drinking water at all times. Like food, the amount of water required by any dog will vary according to his age, activity level, the climate and humidity, and the type of diet being fed.

Until your dog is housebroken:

- Follow a regular feeding schedule.
- Keep your dog's diet consistent.
- Set his food and water dishes down for 15 to 20 minutes, then remove them until the next scheduled meal.
- Do not offer treats or table scraps.

CONFINING YOUR DOG
TO A "DEN"

The next important principle of housebreaking, paper- or litter pan training is based on the dog's den-dwelling instincts. You already know that dogs prefer to keep their dens clean. And since they don't like to soil their living quarters, the best way to teach your dog how to control his body functions is to create a "den" and periodically confine him to it. As negative as this may sound, confinement really isn't cruel at all, especially when it is done properly.

Your dog must never be allowed total freedom in your home until he is completely housebroken, paper- or litter pan trained. Otherwise, you'll be mopping up after him twenty-four hours a day. Draw up a timetable, one that is *humane for the dog* and manageable for you, and adhere to it strictly. You may wish to consult the suggested timetables that begin on page 51. Your dog must learn to stay in his cozy den until it's time to go outside or to his papers or pan, or to have a free period. Once he understands what you want him to do, it will take only a short while until the habit is established. As housebreaking or paper-training progresses and your dog is urinating and defecating where and when he should, he can enjoy progressively longer periods of freedom before being confined again. Remember: *your dog will not require confinement forever, only until he is trained.* And when he finally has the run of your house, he will have earned it with his trustworthy behavior.

A Crate as a "Den"

Before you start housebreaking, paper- or litter pan training, consider buying a wire cage or crate (I use the words "crate" and "cage" interchangeably) with a door for your dog's confinement. Crating is *not* cruel. It is a humane practice used and endorsed by many professional trainers, breeders, handlers, dog show exhibitors, groomers, and veterinarians. Should you hear remarks such as "I wouldn't put *my* dog in a cage like that—it's inhumane," simply remind your unenlightened friends that human babies spend a great deal of time in playpens, and nobody charges their mothers with cruelty for that.

A crate is one of the most useful items you can buy for your dog because it is a home within a home. It becomes the dog's den, a private place where he can be secure and one he will not want to soil. Crating is an excellent way to control your dog overnight and when you are going to be away for a few hours, *not* an entire day. (If you are out of the house for many hours during the day, see "Confinement Without a Crate" at the end of this chapter and "How to Use the 7-Day Program If You Work All Day" on page 37.) You will breathe easier knowing that your puppy can't soil the carpets or chew the furniture while you're sleeping or when he's home alone. It is important, however, not to misuse the crate and make it your dog's private prison; animals that are crated continuously without human contact become depressed.

In addition to housebreaking purposes, a crate is convenient for car travel. You can include your dog in family outings instead of leaving him at home alone or in a boarding kennel. A crated animal feels more secure inside a moving vehicle; he can't jump out of the car and become injured or lost; he's safe from sudden swerves or stops; he can't annoy the passengers or, more importantly, wedge himself between the brake and the driver's foot and cause an accident. My husband and I travel a great deal and, if we are driving, usually take along our dog. She would be terribly unhappy without her crate in hotel and motel rooms. She adapts to strange environments easily because her crate becomes her security blanket. When we plan to be out of the room for a long time, we never shut her up in the crate, but we do leave the crate's door open. When we return, she's always curled up inside her "home away from home," waiting for us.

Crates are made of metal, wood, or high-density polypropylene, but the kind constructed of 6- and 9-gauge or 7- and 11-gauge chrome-plated wire (the lower the gauge, the tougher the wire) is the best choice for housebreaking. It is well ventilated and allows your dog to see everything that's happening around him. Most wire crates fold down and carry easily (some also have carrying handles), allowing you to move them from room to room, so your dog can be where the action is even though he's confined. *Confinement does not mean isolation.* It is acceptable—indeed, desirable—to place the crate in or near communal rooms, such as the kitchen or the family room. Dogs of all ages need human companionship, and if it is denied them, they will become lonely and frustrated.

The correct size is important: your crate should be just big enough for your puppy or grown dog to stand up in without touching the top, and comfortable enough for him to turn around and lie down in, and to stretch his legs without being cramped. It is inhumane to confine a dog to a crate that is too small; on the other hand, the cage must not be so large that your dog can relieve himself at one end and sleep at the other. He'll end up walking or sitting in urine or feces, and you'll have a messy dog and crate to clean!

You can buy a crate at most pet stores and megastores like Wal-Mart and Target, from concessionaires at dog shows, over the Internet, or from mail-order pet-supplies catalogs (some names and addresses are listed at the end of this book). The cost depends on quality and size and generally averages from $55 for a crate 24-by-18-inches wide by 21 inches high (suitable for small breeds), to about $85 for one 30-by-21-inches wide by 24 inches high (suitable for medium-sized breeds), to about $120 for one 42-by-28-inches wide by 32-inches high (to accommodate large breeds). Even bigger crates are also available for tall and massive breeds, such as Great Danes, Saint Bernards, Newfoundlands, and Irish Wolfhounds.

Buy the best crate you can afford; one that is sturdy will last a lifetime. (You can also build your own crate if you are handy with tools.) Even the costliest crate is worth the money when you consider the expense of replacing a soiled carpet. If you have a puppy that's going to grow a lot and want to get the most for your money, buy a crate that will fit him when he becomes an adult, and temporarily block off the excess space with a divider panel designed to reduce the size of the cage, or a plywood partition. One of the differences between top-quality and lower-quality metal crates is the spacing and rigidity of the bars. Close, durable wire spacing ensures stability and security. A rambunctious puppy should never be able to wedge his head or paws unintentionally between the bars. See that the latch is secure enough so that your dog cannot paw it open.

Most wire crates come with removable galvanized pans that are easy to clean and disinfect. It's okay to put down a towel, small blanket, or washable bath mat if you don't want your puppy to sleep on the metal pan, as long as this does not encourage him to chew it or to urinate or defecate on it, but if you are paper-training instead of housebreaking your dog, *never* line the crate with newspaper. A few favorite toys and chew bones will keep your dog entertained while he's inside. Once the dog is housebroken, you can then buy or make a double-sided fleece mat to make the cage bottom more comfortable and warm.

Try to get your puppy accustomed to his crate *before* you begin the 7-day program. Put him in it for short intervals during the day while you stay close by to reassure him that being locked up for a little while isn't the end of the world and let him go in and out at will. (In the case of puppies too young to begin the housebreaking schedule outlined in this book, it's a good idea to place a crate with the door open in the temporary "den" as outlined on page 11.) You should be able to reach into the crate and touch him at any time.

The first night your puppy spends shut up in his crate may be troublesome. He will be lonely and may begin to whimper for attention. Comfort him with gentle words, but do not take him out. If you give in to his mournful sounds, the puppy will quickly learn that crying brings him attention and possibly freedom, and he will do it every night. Ignore him. It's distressing to look at that unhappy little face and hear those plaintive sobs, I know, but your puppy must learn to control himself. If you can harden your heart for only seven days, you and your puppy will be happier in the long run. Pretty soon, he'll be able to keep his den clean and not relieve himself where he sleeps. He may make a mistake on the first night and possibly on the next few nights, but he will quickly learn control. Be considerate and take your puppy out early in the morning so he can relieve himself. If your puppy soils his crate, take him out of it, rush him outdoors, point out his toilet area, and praise him lavishly the next time he goes there. *Don't ever let your puppy sit in a crate that contains urine or feces, and never put him back inside one that is dirty.*

Make your dog's confinement in his crate a pleasant experience.

Never let him associate confinement with punishment. Never speak harshly to him while he's confined or discipline him then. *Never crate him for extended periods, especially if you work long hours during the day.* His crate must be his refuge, a secure and cozy resting place, not his prison cell. After your dog is housebroken or paper-trained and no longer requires confinement when you are home, leave the crate door open so he can go inside when he wants to sleep or be alone, or when he's ill. And when your puppy goes in his crate of his own choice, he should not be pestered by children or by other pets. Children must also understand that the crate is the puppy's "private room" and not something for them to play in.

Confinement Without a Crate

If you do not wish to crate your dog, especially if you go out of the house during the day, you can still create a "den" by blocking off a small area in the kitchen, bathroom, hallway, or in any other room that is easy to clean. The size of the den will vary with each puppy. Some dogs can keep an area the size of an entire kitchen or a bathroom scrupulously clean, while others would sleep in one corner and relieve themselves in another. You can start by confining your dog to a small kitchen, pantry, or bathroom to take advantage of his den-dwelling instincts—the desire to keep his quarters clean—but if he urinates or defecates in that small area, decrease the size of the den *immediately* with cardboard partitions until he's confined to an area that meets his needs. You may end up with a den that is 24 by 36 inches or even smaller, but the *right* amount of space will keep your dog from soiling during the training program.

If you are able to use a small bathroom, kitchen, or pantry, you can close off the "den" with an adjustable pet gate. The most popular kind has a 32-inch-high hardwood frame with vinyl-coated wire mesh that cannot be chewed through. No installation is required because the gate adjusts from about 26- to 42-inches wide and conforms to nearly every type of doorway in a home. *Never* use a gate with spaces large enough to trap your puppy's head or paws. And never confine your dog in a small space behind a closed door. You'll only upset him and promote behavior problems. Make his short confinement period as cozy as possible so that he will not bark or cry when he's left alone. This is a particular problem in apartment houses, where whining and barking dogs can annoy neighbors.

If you go to work every day, read more about confinement without a crate under "How to Use the 7-Day Program If You Work All Day" on page 37.

HOUSEBREAKING

Training your dog to urinate and defecate outdoors is easy when you establish a pattern. Dogs are creatures of habit: they like to eat, to sleep, and to relieve themselves (away from their feeding and sleeping places) on a regular schedule, so it's important to establish good habits from the start. The first step, as you already know, is to put your dog on a nutritious and regulated diet. He should eat from one to three meals a day depending on his age, consuming the same amount of food at the same times every day.

Next, since you want to teach your dog to relieve himself outside, you must establish a schedule to give him regular and reasonably spaced opportunities to urinate and defecate where and when you want him to. Most dogs naturally develop the habit of relieving themselves outdoors when they are given ample opportunities to do so. Just be sure your puppy goes outside often enough. Some typical schedules for dogs of different age ranges begin on page 51. These can help you organize a 7-day pattern that will be compatible with your lifestyle and result in successful housebreaking. Investing just seven days in consistent scheduling seems a small price to pay for years of pleasure with a disciplined canine companion.

A note before proceeding further: Don't become disappointed or discouraged if you cannot *totally* housebreak your puppy in seven days. Every puppy is different; some may take longer to train. You have established the fundamentals; stick to the schedule for a little longer and give your puppy a chance to understand them.

Leash-Training Is a Must in Most Cases

If you don't have a fenced-in yard or if you live in a city, your puppy will have to be leash-trained before you begin the 7-day program. The best way to accomplish this is to get the puppy accustomed to wearing a collar right away. Buy a serviceable, lightweight collar. Don't spend a lot of money if your pup is just a baby; most breeds, except the tiny toys, grow out of several collars as they mature. Start with something practical and replace it as soon as it becomes too small.

When you first put the collar around your puppy's neck, he will probably turn somersaults trying to remove it, so stay with him. Let him wear the collar for 10- to 15-minute intervals several times each day while you keep praising him and telling him he's the cutest thing on four legs. Your goal is to get the puppy used to wearing the collar in gradual stages before you attach a lead and try to walk him.

The next step is to snap a leash onto the collar and let the puppy drag it around the room wherever *he* wants to go. Don't pick up the leash or guide the puppy the first few times; just stay nearby to extricate him from any entanglements. After a few sessions, try holding the leash loosely in your hand and follow the puppy around the room. Then try to lead the puppy where *you* want to go. Most likely he'll want nothing to do with moving forward and may even pull backwards and roll on the floor. Keep calm. Bend down, call your puppy's name, and say "Come" in your most tempting voice. If he does not step forward, give the leash a gentle pull. Never jerk the leash sharply, for that will only frighten him. When he toddles to you, praise him lavishly, then walk ahead with the leash in your hand. Repeat these steps until the puppy learns to walk beside you. If you can accomplish this soon after the puppy enters your home, he can be completely leash-trained before he is old enough to be housebroken.

City Dogs

Dogs on city streets should be leashed and under control at all times. Laws concerning dogs are becoming stricter and are being more rigorously enforced; it is the duty of urban dog owners to become familiar with local leash and scoop laws and to observe them.

During the 7-day training period, take your dog out only to urinate and defecate, and not for any other reason. Once he's housebroken he can go for long walks, but right now you want him to associate going outside to the street with the acts of urination and defecation. Do train him to relieve himself as close to home as possible, so you won't have to trudge very far when it's pouring rain or snowing, or late at night.

As soon as you go outside, walk or carry your puppy to the curb so that he learns from day one that this is the correct toilet area. If he squats and starts to go on the sidewalk, carry him or gently pull him to the edge of the street and praise him warmly when he finishes there. He'll soon get your message. *Never* let your dog relieve himself on your neighbor's lawn, in children's playgrounds, or in recreational areas.

A female dog always squats to urinate, so she's fairly easy to curb-train. But as a male dog matures, he will begin to raise his hind leg and aim at vertical "targets." This male urination pattern is part of the ritual of territorial marking in which, among other things, the lingering scent communicates his presence to other males in the area. Be considerate, therefore, about the spots you let your male use: curbstones, fireplugs, and telephone poles can be acceptable places, but never let your dog christen young trees, automobiles (the acid in his urine will corrode paint and chrome), fences, mailboxes, or ornamental plants or shrubbery. And don't forget to scoop up feces. Despite scoop laws, excessive fecal matter is a major problem of large cities these days because many owners refuse to clean up after their dogs defecate. It's distasteful when people have to scrape your dog's feces off their shoes, and it will make you very unpopular with your neighbors.

Starting the 7-Day Program When You Are at Home All Day

The night before you begin the housebreaking program, take your dog out and be sure he relieves himself completely. Remove his collar and put him in his crate or confine him to his "den" (his crate or a blocked-off space in the kitchen or any other room that is easy to clean) for the night. His blanket or bath mat and a few favorite toys will help to console him.

If you plan to crate your puppy during the night, place his cage near your bed so you can take him out first thing in the morning. *He must go out as soon as you wake up.* Don't take a shower or put on the coffee. In fact, during the training period, it's a good idea to lay out some comfortable clothes before you go to bed, along with shoes you can slip into quickly, your puppy's collar and leash, and your keys. As soon as the alarm sounds, get out of bed, get dressed quickly, take your dog out of the crate, and carry him outside for the first couple of days to avoid accidents.

Never put your puppy out in the yard by himself, even if it is fenced in. Carry or walk him to the area you want him to use, and let him sniff around for a preferred spot. Don't rush him. Sniffing is important to some dogs to stimulate elimination. Walk back and forth a little as you say "Go potty," "Business," or something similar (use the same phrase each time), repeating it over and over until the dog relieves himself. The moment he does, praise him and tell him how clever he is, then bring him back indoors. The puppy can have a little play period in the kitchen while you prepare breakfast, but *never* let him loose in the house without supervision at this time.

Give him breakfast. Pick up his dish after 15 to 20 minutes and give him a drink of water. During the training period, remember, water is being restricted by time, not by quantity, so give him all he wants to drink. Fifteen to 20 minutes later, snap the leash onto his collar, say "Let's go out," and take him to the same spot. Always re-

turn to the same toilet area, because the odors that linger from previous visits should remind your dog why he's there. Say "Go potty" or "Business," and praise him enthusiastically when he does his duty, then return indoors. If nothing happens, however, bring him back inside, confine him in the crate for about 15 minutes, then take him out once more. He *must* learn to associate these first outings with the acts of urination and/or defecation, and, if he simply walks aimlessly about, come back inside and confine him for another 15 to 20 minutes before you try again. You may have to do this three or four times on the first few mornings, but once you learn how his "internal clock" functions, you'll get your timing straight.

When the puppy does relieve himself after breakfast, he can have another supervised free period before being confined until his next meal or outing, when you will repeat these same steps again. The length of supervised free periods depends on a puppy's age. Once yours can handle a 30-minute period with no accidents, give him more freedom by increasing his free time to 45 minutes, and so on. Your goal is to increase his free periods gradually until he needs to be confined (during the training period) *only* when you are away from home. He does not have to spend all his supervised free time in one room, because he needs to investigate and to mingle with family members (and other pets if you have them) as much as possible. Just don't let him discover your antique oriental rug until he has completely relieved himself. If the puppy regresses, it's back to square one: start the training program *from the beginning* once more.

A puppy will relieve himself many times during the day, especially if he is very young, and you must be prepared to take him out:

- Immediately after he wakes up in the morning.
- 15 to 20 minutes after every meal and drink of water.

■ After he wakes up from a nap.
■ After extreme excitement or long play periods.
■ The last thing at night.

Between these times, stay alert for signs that your puppy is looking to relieve himself—actions such as whining, acting restless, sniffing the floor, or going around in circles. The time interval between "indicating" and "doing" is very short in young puppies but gets longer with age. When you see him doing these things, try to distract him, then pick him up (if you can) and rush him outside to his toilet area. You may be going out eight to ten times the first few days, but once the puppy settles into his routine, he should not have to go out more than four to six times a day, depending on his age.

Stick to a strict schedule. The more conscientious you are now, the more successful the training will be. It takes patience to make your puppy understand what you want him to do, but he will adapt to your schedule eventually. *There will be accidents, of course; that's part of raising puppies.* When your dog makes a mistake in the house, never abuse him physically. Correct him humanely. No punishment! The words "No" and "Bad dog" are the only corrections you need. How you say these words can convey your displeasure very effectively. This subject is covered more fully under "Corrective Training Is Easy . . . with a Little Patience and Love," on page 59.

Always go outside with your puppy during the training period, even if your yard is fenced in. You want to see when and where he relieves himself, and your enthusiastic praise will encourage him. Once the puppy is completely housebroken, it will not be necessary to accompany him outdoors. However, if you live in the city, or if you do not have an enclosed yard, you must always go out with your dog. *Never let him roam free.*

How to Use the 7-Day Program If You Work All Day

You can housebreak or paper-train your dog even if you work all day. Your routine will be the same, only you will adjust the dog's feeding and walking times, supervised free periods, and confinement to conform with your work hours. To help you establish a successful pattern, consult the suggested schedules for dogs of different ages, beginning on page 51.

The night before you begin the housebreaking program, take your dog out and be sure he relieves himself completely. Remove his collar and put him in his crate or confine him to his kitchen or bathroom "den" for the night. His blanket or bath mat and a few favorite toys will make him more comfortable. If you plan to crate your puppy during the night, place his cage near your bed so you can take him out first thing in the morning. Plan to get up a little earlier than usual for the first few days, in order to give you and your dog some extra time to settle into the routine. As soon as the alarm sounds, get out of bed promptly, get dressed (don't shower or put on the coffee yet), and carry your dog outside to avoid accidents. Never send your puppy out into the yard by himself, even if it is fenced in. Take him to the area you want him to use, and let him sniff around for a preferred spot. Walk back and forth a little as you say "Go potty," "Business," or something similar. Use the same phrase each time, repeating it over and over until the dog relieves himself. The moment he does, praise him lavishly and bring him back indoors. Give the puppy a little play period in the kitchen while you prepare breakfast, but *never* let him loose in the house without supervision at this time.

Feed him his breakfast, then pick up his dish after 15 to 20 minutes and give him a drink of water. Fifteen to 20 minutes later, snap the leash onto his collar, say "Let's go out," and take him to the same spot. Say "Go potty" and praise him enthusiastically when he relieves himself, then return indoors. If nothing happens, bring him back inside, confine him in the crate for about 15 minutes, then take him out once more. He must learn to associate these first outings with the acts of urination and/or defecation. If he just meanders about, or behaves as if this is a play period, come back inside and confine him for another 15- to 20-minute period before you try again. You may have to go out three to four times on the first few mornings to determine his natural excretory habits, but once you learn them, you'll get your timing straight.

Just before you leave for work, if no one else will be at home, confine your dog to his den for the day. If you are going to be out of the house for a considerable time period, *do not* crate the dog for the entire day. Since most puppies cannot control their bladder or bowels for eight- to ten-hour-long stretches, don't expect your dog to sit alone in his crate for the entire day and not relieve himself. More importantly, you don't want to come home and find him sitting in a cage soiled with urine and feces. In this case, it would be more humane to block off a small area in the kitchen or bathroom for his den.

Leave plenty of safe toys and things to chew to keep him entertained, but avoid too much rawhide during the 7-day program; it makes him thirsty, and his water is being restricted. Unless the weather is extremely hot or humid and you have no air-conditioning, you should not have to leave water down during the 7-day period while you are at work. If you do leave water, though, give him only a small amount or, better yet, leave a few ice cubes to melt in a dish.

When it's time to leave for work, go promptly without any emotional farewell. Don't make a dramatic exhibition out of leaving, and never show your puppy that his whimpers will postpone your departure.

You can decrease your puppy's confinement and restraint time if you can get home for lunch, or arrange with a neighbor, friend, or professional dog walker to stop in at noon to give him water and walk him. But if you must leave the puppy alone all day, come *straight* home after work. No "happy hour" with colleagues during the training period. Greet the puppy animatedly and make a big fuss over him no matter what his den looks like. It's normal to find a puddle or a mess when you first begin the training program. Just don't scold your puppy if you find one. Delayed punishment is *not* effective, as dogs do not understand discipline for mistakes that occurred in the past. Instead, put on his collar as fast as you can, say "Let's go out," and *rush* outside. Once you return indoors, pick up any dirty papers and clean the den, if

necessary, and resume the feeding, walking, free-period, and confinement schedule until bedtime.

Keep your puppy's feeding and walking times as consistent as possible during the training period—and permanently as much as possible—to avoid throwing him off schedule. In other words, during the seven days (and for several weeks after until the dog's habits are established) don't feed him at 7:30 A.M. on weekdays and then sleep late on weekends, and don't confine him all day while you are at work and then take him out constantly on Saturday and Sunday afternoons.

Eventually you will return home one night to find no mistakes. And when that happens, you can celebrate.

Dogs want to be with their masters, not isolated from them, so it's important to give your puppy plenty of exercise and attention while you are at home so he does not become discontented and bored while you are gone. He should be well exercised before and after confinement. Get up earlier or allot time after work to cuddle your puppy and give him a little romp. Once he's completely housebroken, take him for long walks or a run in the park. Your dog should not object to being confined if he's toned up and contented. This time spent playing with and loving your puppy will be repaid by his faithfulness and loving companionship.

The Importance of Cleanliness and Good Grooming

One subject that most pet owners (and even some trainers) do not associate with housebreaking is cleanliness and good grooming. When a dog's paws or the hair on his rear end become soiled with urine or feces, when he goes ungroomed or unbathed for any length of time, or when his environment is not kept clean, he often becomes depressed and relieves himself in the house (if he is housebroken) or away from his papers (if he is paper-trained). His sense of smell may eventually become so accustomed to his excretory odors that he is unable to distinguish between his den and where he relieves himself.

Keep your dog clean, fresh smelling, and well groomed at all times. If he requires complicated clipping and trimming, you'll most likely have to have him coiffed and manicured by a professional. But between his regular appointments, brush and comb him frequently and clean any soiled areas on his body with a dry or foam shampoo. A clean dog looks and feels good, and regular grooming sessions serve other purposes, such as promoting a better relationship between dog and owner, and giving the owner a chance to spot potential health problems.

I once had an interesting experience with a male puppy in one of my Miniature Poodle litters. Jonathan's dam was extremely fastidious about keeping her babies clean in the nest. As soon as they reached five weeks of age, I started handling and brushing them gently and keeping them groomed and clean. We kept Jonathan as a show prospect until, at five months of age, he grew an inch over the accepted AKC size limit. So he went off to new, caring owners (we thought), beautifully groomed and completely housebroken. Imagine my surprise when his owners telephoned many months later to say that Jonathan was messing all over their house. I asked to see the dog and was shocked when they brought him back. Jonathan had not been groomed since he left our home, and he was a dirty, smelly mass of tangles. After a bath and a trim, I sent him home with instructions for hair care and a housebreaking retraining program. I thought things were fine until several months later when the owners called again to say that unless I returned their money, they were going to place Jonathan in an animal shelter because he was impossible to housebreak. I shouldn't have to tell you that when they returned the poor dog, he was again ungroomed and smelled to high heaven. Jonathan came home to stay, and from the moment he was bathed and groomed regularly, the dog never made a mistake in our house.

A Word of Advice

By the time your puppy is sixteen weeks of age, he should be able to go through the night without having to relieve himself. However, if a healthy puppy urinates and defecates before going to bed yet continually soils his crate at night during the training program, it may mean that he has not developed the muscle control he needs. Postpone the training for a week or two. You might also try, for a short time, going to bed later than usual or getting up during the night to take the puppy out.

PAPER-TRAINING AND
LITTER PAN TRAINING

Paper-training is useful:

- If you own a small dog and live in an apartment.
- If you are somewhat advanced in life or handicapped and it is not easy to walk your dog.
- For very young puppies that do not have complete muscle control of their bladder and bowels, or that cannot go outdoors until they are completely immunized (check with your veterinarian about which vaccine combinations are required for your area).
- For older dogs that can't walk long distances or whose medical conditions cause increased urination.
- If you work long hours and your dog is at home alone.

One of the biggest mistakes made by pet owners is to paper-train a puppy when the actual goal is to housebreak the pet. Paper-training is *not* the first step toward outdoor training. It is primarily for dogs that will *always* relieve themselves indoors on paper, and should be avoided if you ultimately expect your dog to urinate and defecate outside. There are exceptions, of course. The first is the young puppy that has not gained complete muscle control or that cannot go outside because he is not fully immunized. In both cases, the use of newspapers is only temporary. Combining newspaper and outdoor training for more than a few weeks often creates confusion for young puppies about where to relieve themselves. If you don't switch to a rigid walking schedule as soon as your puppy is able to go outdoors, he may refuse to urinate and defecate there but wait until he comes back in the house to his newspapers to relieve himself, or to the place where his newspapers used to be. Then you'll really confuse the puppy if you reprimand him for going on newspapers when you previously praised him for the same action.

Suppose you have a puppy you intend to housebreak but that is not yet fully immunized or that cannot go for any length of time without emptying his bladder or bowels. The best solution is *not* to formally paper-train him but to confine him to a papered "nursery" area in your kitchen until he is old enough to go outdoors. Since you can't watch him constantly, restrict him to a small area or put him in a roomy puppy pen. The confinement area should be covered with

newspapers, but you're just not going to praise your puppy for using them. As soon as the puppy is totally immunized or has better control over his urination and defecation, remove the newspapers completely and take him outdoors. Many training manuals tell you that the best way to switch a young puppy from paper-training to housebreaking is gradually to reduce the size of his papers as you gradually move them closer to the outside door. Personally, I believe the best way is to immediately supplant the old training with the new.

Take the puppy out and stay with him, no matter how long it takes, until he does what you want. If your puppy is stubborn and refuses to void outdoors, take along a piece of newspaper (preferably one that contains the scent of his excrement) to help give him the idea that this is the right place. Your neighbors may think you are bizarre, but this usually produces the hoped-for result.

The second exception is when you work long hours and *must* teach your dog to use newspapers in conjunction with going outdoors. This is a real problem because you must be resigned to the fact that your dog can use his newspapers at any time, not just when you're away. If you envision a perfectly paper-trained and housebroken dog in this case, you are going to be disappointed. Paper-training tells your dog that it is not wrong for him to relieve himself indoors, so you cannot scold him when he urinates or defecates in the house when you're at home.

How to Paper-Train

The suggested schedules for paper-training are the same as those for housebreaking, on pages 51–56. The difference is that you will be placing your dog on newspapers indoors to relieve himself instead of taking him outside. If you follow these schedules carefully, you can paper-train your dog in seven days.

Select a corner in one room—the kitchen, the bathroom, or even a hallway—that will serve as the dog's indoor toilet area. It should be a place where accidents will be easy to clean up and where your dog can relieve himself without disrupting the family's routine. Keep the toilet area away from his sleeping and feeding spots. Cover a 3-by-4-foot area of the floor with a cut-open plastic trash bag spread with six to eight layers of newspaper. You are papering a larger toilet area than your dog normally needs, but this will make it easier for him to locate the paper at first. You might want to tape down the corners of the papers to keep them from sliding. It's very important to put the papers in the same location every time. Take your dog there first thing every morning, after each meal or drink of water, after each nap, after exercise or play periods, and before bedtime (as outlined on the housebreaking schedules), and whenever he seems to be fidgety or looking for a place to urinate or defecate. Speak to him softly and tell him to use his paper. Every time he performs his duty, praise him enthusiastically to let him know he's done the right thing, then reward him with a little freedom. Follow the same routine every day. If you catch him voiding off the paper, pick him up immediately and carry him there. Correct him humanely and never punish him.

The newspapers should be changed regularly, but save one soiled sheet and place it on top of the fresh supply. The scent of his excrement should draw him back to the same spot. As soon as your dog learns to relieve himself on the papers, put him down a short distance away from them after he eats or drinks, call him to "Come" and "Go potty," and let him walk to the newpapers. This is the time that you would be walking him outdoors if you were housebreaking him, and it's important to the dog to learn to walk to the paper soon after he finishes eating or drinking. Within a few days your puppy should pick out a favorite spot and start heading there automatically, and you can begin to reduce the size of the papered space. It should never be smaller than the size of a single non-tabloid newspaper opened up. Make sure it's several layers thick for absorbency. Should your dog start urinating and defecating off the paper at any time, you'll have to start the training process over again.

Puppy "Piddle Pads," available at pet stores, are an alternative to newspaper. These have several absorbent layers with leak-proof bottoms and contain special scents that attract puppies to "go" where the pads are.

Gradually increase your puppy's free periods as the training progresses successfully until he does not need to be confined while you are at home.

Litter Pan Training

Training a small or medium-sized dog to relieve himself in a cat litter pan is a practical alternative to paper training. It's also more humane for geriatric dogs that can't walk long distances, or dogs that suffer from certain medical problems that cause increased urination. Additionally, a tray filled with shredded newspapers or absorbent litter (your pet-supplies dealer can advise which type is best) is more pleasing to the eye than a pile of soiled papers on the kitchen or bathroom floor. A basic, rectangular box is all you need. These vary greatly in size from small to jumbo (for multiple cats), with high or low sides. Consider your dog's size and select a box that will give him room to move around comfortably—he should be able to eliminate and still have some clean areas to stand on. The best type of litter pan is made of heavy plastic so it can be washed regularly with soap and hot water and disinfected when necessary.

The schedules for litter pan training are the same as those for housebreaking or paper-training. Instead of taking your dog outside, however, you will take him to the litter pan to relieve himself. As with housebreaking, you must take your dog to the tray the first thing every morning, after each meal or drink of water, after each nap, after exercise or play periods, before bedtime (as outlined on the schedules), and whenever he seems to be searching for a place to urinate or defecate.

A good way to entice your dog to use the tray is to place shredded newspapers previously stained with his urine in it, or to leave a small amount of his feces in the pan. The scent will help remind him what he's supposed to do. The first few times you take him out of his crate or den, carry him to the tray and hold him there for a few minutes. Let him sniff the paper or litter while you say "Go potty" in your most inviting voice. Praise him enthusiastically if he urinates or defecates. If nothing happens, put him back in his crate for another 10 to 15 minutes, then carry him to the tray again. If that doesn't produce results, crate him for another 15 minutes. Don't hold him in the tray for more than 5 minutes without success. He must learn to go to the tray whenever he feels the urge to urinate or defecate. If your dog balks at defecating in the tray at first, as a last resort, you can insert an infant glycerine suppository into his rectum and hold him there for a few minutes until it works. (An infant suppository will not harm the dog.) But do this only *once or twice* until the dog associates the litter pan with the process of elimination. Don't make it a habit.

To control odors, remove solid wastes immediately. If they are in clay litter, scoop them up and flush them down the toilet or otherwise dispose of them. Remove any soiled paper after each use and replace it with clean paper. Even though dogs are attracted to the scent of excrement, they don't like to walk on paper or litter saturated with urine or feces or to step into a disgustingly dirty tray. Shredded newspaper can get very smelly when saturated with urine, and, in addition to the daily scooping, the box will need a thorough scrubbing at least once a week with hot water and a mild detergent, such as a dishwashing liquid, followed by a thorough rinsing and drying. Do not, however, use strong-smelling cleaning products when washing the litter box, as this may cause your dog to avoid it.

CHOOSING THE SCHEDULE
THAT'S RIGHT FOR YOU

Here are some sample schedules to follow if you want to house-break your dog in seven days. Schedule No. 1 is for owners who are at home all day with 4- to 6-month-old puppies. Schedule No. 2 is for owners who work all day and who have 4- to 6-month-old puppies. Schedule No. 3 is for owners who are at home all day with 6- to 12-month-old puppies. Schedule No. 4 is for owners who work all day and who have 6- to 12-month-old puppies. Schedule Nos. 5 and 6 are general guidelines to follow once dogs are housebroken.

Schedule Nos. 1 through 4 are general timetables; not everyone will be able to follow them precisely, because each dog has his own particular habits, as does his owner. For instance, some dogs urinate and defecate right after they have been fed, while others wait one-half hour or longer after eating to relieve themselves. Choose the appropriate schedule to use as a model, and once you learn how long nature needs to take its course, you can adapt it to fit your individual needs. Just be sure you are consistent. And I mean *consistent*, like clockwork.

Notice that 4- to 6-month-old puppies are given 30 minutes of free time in any given period, while those from 6 to 12 months are allowed 45 minutes of freedom. A 5-month-old puppy may be so dependable that you can give him 45 minutes of freedom, or a 9-month-old puppy may be worthy of an hour-long free period. As your puppy matures and the training progresses, give him longer and longer periods of freedom, until he needs confinement only when you go out. The schedules apply *only* during the 7-day program (and possibly a few more days if your puppy needs additional training time), not for the rest of his life. Every member of the family should adhere to them. Consistency from the entire family will speed up the training and make your dog a better-adjusted and happier pet.

SCHEDULE NO. 1

General Timetable for 4- to 6-Month-Old Puppy Eating 3 Meals a Day; Owner at Home All Day

a.m.	
7:00	Wake up. Go out.*
7:10–7:30	Free period in kitchen.
7:30	Food and water.
8:00	Go out.
8:15–8:45	Free period in kitchen.
8:45	Confine (in crate or small blocked-off area in kitchen or bathroom).
Noon	Food and water.
p.m.	
12:30	Go out.
12:45–1:15	Free period in kitchen.
1:15	Confine.
5:00	Food and water.

p.m.

5:30	Go out.
5:45–6:15	Free period in kitchen.
6:15	Confine.
8:00	Water
8:15	Go out.
8:30–9:00	Free period in kitchen.
9:00	Confine.
11:00	Go out. Confine overnight.

SCHEDULE NO. 2

**General Timetable for 4- to 6-Month-Old Puppy
Eating 3 Meals a Day; Owner Working During Day**

a.m.

7:00	Wake up. Go out.*
7:10–7:30	Free period in kitchen.
7:30	Food and water.
8:00	Go out. Confine when owner leaves (*not* in crate for entire day, but in small blocked-off area in kitchen or bathroom). Leave safe toys to keep dog entertained. Try to come home for lunch or arrange for neighbor or friend to water and walk dog at noon.

p.m.

6:00	Go out as soon as owner returns home.
6:10–6:30	Free period in kitchen.
6:30	Food and water.
7:00	Go out.
7:15	Confine.
9:00	Small amount of food and water.
9:30	Go out.
9:40–10:30	Free period in kitchen.
10:30–11:00	Go out. Confine overnight.

SCHEDULE NO. 3

General Timetable for 6- to 12-Month-Old Puppy Eating 2 Meals a Day; Owner at Home All Day

a.m.

7:00	Wake up. Go out.*
7:15–8:00	Free period in kitchen.
8:00	Food and water.
8:30	Go out.
8:45–9:30	Free period in kitchen.
9:30	Confine (in crate or small blocked-off area).

p.m.

12:30	Water.
12:45	Go out.
1:00–1:45	Free period in kitchen.
1:45	Confine.
6:00	Food and water.
6:30	Go out.
6:45–7:30	Free period in kitchen.
7:30	Confine.
10:30–11:00	Go out. Confine overnight.

SCHEDULE NO. 4

General Timetable for 6- to 12-Month-Old Puppy Eating 2 Meals a Day; Owner Working During Day

a.m.

7:00	Wake up. Go out.*
7:10–7:30	Free period in kitchen.
7:30	Food and water.
8:00	Go out. Confine when owner leaves (*not* in crate for entire day but in small blocked-off area in kitchen or bathroom). Leave safe toys to keep dog entertained. Try to come home for lunch or arrange for neighbor to water and walk dog at noon.

p.m.

6:00	Go out as soon as owner returns home.
6:15–7:00	Free period in kitchen.
7:00	Food and water.
7:30	Go out.
7:45–8:30	Free period in kitchen.
8:30	Confine.
10:30–11:00	Go out. Confine overnight.

SCHEDULE NO. 5

General Timetable for Housebroken Adult Dog Eating 1 or 2 Meals a Day; Owner at Home All Day

a.m.

7:00	Wake up. Go out.*
8:00	Food. Unlimited water supply during day.
8:30	Go out.

p.m.

1:00	Go out.
5:30	Food (if dog eats 2 meals per day).
6:00	Go out.
11:00	Go out. Bedtime. Remove water during night.

SCHEDULE NO. 6

General Timetable for Housebroken Adult Dog
Eating 1 or 2 Meals a Day; Owner Working During Day

a.m.

7:00	Wake up. Go out.*
7:30	Food. Unlimited water supply during day.
8:00	Go out. When owner leaves, confine dog if necessary (*not* in crate for entire day).

p.m.

6:00	Go out as soon as owner returns home.
6:30–7:00	Food (if dog eats 2 meals per day).
7:30–7:45	Go out (if dog eats 2 meals per day).
11:00	Go out. Bedtime. Remove water during night.

Note: If you are training your dog to eliminate indoors, on all schedules where "Go out" is indicated, substitute "Go to paper or litter pan."

THE POWER OF PRAISE

Dogs are highly motivated by praise. Praise is the most effective way to show your dog that you are pleased with him. It is a crucial element in any type of canine training, and it should be administered in generous doses. Every time your dog does something right, especially if he's a puppy, flatter his ego with plenty of praise. Let him know that what he has done has pleased you tremendously. Make a huge fuss as you say "Good dog," "Good boy," or "Good girl" enthusiastically. You don't need to use the same word or phrase always; your tone of voice will convey your enthusiasm. And express your pleasure with your touch, too. Your hands should always communicate affection. Stroke your dog lovingly as a reward. Each time you express your approval, you will be positively reinforcing the behavior you praise. Dogs are show-offs and love being the center of attention. They want to hear how wonderful and how smart and how beautiful they are. Just watch how eager your dog is to please after a few kind words.

Some trainers recommend the use of treats as a reward, especially after a dog relieves himself outdoors or on paper indoors, but I don't believe it's a good idea to use food as an incentive during the 7-day training period. Your dog must learn to control his bladder and his bowels and to relieve himself when and where you want him to, not when and where he feels like it, or when he gets a treat. Otherwise he'll be more interested in snacking than learning. Besides, it is not necessary to use food to bribe a dog that is eager to work as hard as he can for guidance and praise from his master. (Give treats when the 7-day training period is over, of course.)

Once you understand the power of praise and use it consistently, combined with humane correction for mistakes, you are making progress toward sharing your life with a happy dog—one that has not been intimidated into being an obedient and trustworthy animal.

CORRECTIVE TRAINING IS EASY...
WITH A LITTLE PATIENCE
AND LOVE

Discipline is one of the most important aspects of any training program, yet it is one of the most troublesome and least understood. Housebreaking behavior is not inherited; it is learned, and immediate and consistent discipline is one of the most important ways owners teach correct conduct to their dogs. Discipline, from the Latin *discipulus*, or "pupil," is training and instruction that is intended to produce a specific pattern of behavior. Discipline is a teaching tool, *not* a punishment that inflicts pain or suffering as a penalty for an offense. Physical punishment causes fear and anxiety, and actually inhibits learning. In the case of housebreaking or paper-training, punishment will definitely slow down the process. Though constant hitting, slapping, or shouting may make your dog obey to avoid your anger, *they are abuse*. Such negative actions will affect the dog's personality and behavior and may make him despise you. And each time you reach down to touch your dog, he will cringe in fear, not knowing if you're going to stroke him or strike him.

It is normal for your dog to make a mistake or two during the 7-day training period and even afterward. The most effective time to administer discipline is to catch the dog in the act ... and *only* then, not after you find an accident that you did not see happen. If you do witness misbehavior, yell "NO!" and try to distract him by making noise. You can make a great attention-getter by dropping some pennies in an empty soda can and sealing the top with tape; the noise produced by shaking the can should be enough to distract the dog. Pick up your dog and carry him outside. If he's too heavy to carry, grab him by the collar and rush him outdoors to his toilet area. Your intent is to startle the dog so he will stop whatever he's doing indoors and finish relieving himself outside. Once he does, praise him lavishly. The object of these actions is to produce a response pattern such as "When I make a mistake in the house, I get disciplined; but when I go outdoors, I am praised."

The only corrections you will ever need are the words "No" and "Bad dog" said in a firm voice. *Never* rub your dog's nose in his urine or feces, and never strike him with your hand or with a rolled-up newspaper, or abuse him physically in any way. Never call your dog by name or command him to "Come" when you intend to administer discipline. A dog should always associate his name and the command "Come" with pleasant experiences.

If your dog continues to make mistakes, take steps to reduce the chance of misconduct by changing his walking or papering schedule, taking him outside or to his papers more often, or giving him less freedom in the house.

DOGS CAN SMELL ODORS
EVEN WHEN YOU CAN'T

During the training period, and for a short time afterward, your dog may have an occasional accident indoors. It is your responsibility to clean the mistake immediately and to deodorize the area to remove any lingering scent. If you clean but forget about deodorizing, your dog will still be able to smell the urine and fecal odors (even though you may not), and he will return to the site of his error and use that same spot again and again. The sense of smell is extremely keen in dogs, many times greater than in humans, and dogs are strongly attracted to the smell of excrement. In the house or out-doors, they prefer to urinate and defecate in the exact place where they or other dogs have gone before. It's their way of marking territory, and it is especially common in male dogs.

Odor problems are generally caused by ammonia, mercaptans, and other chemicals and gases emitted from urine and feces. Fresh urine has hardly any smell, but once it's been deposited onto a surface, it starts to decay. In the first stage of decay, the urea in the urine breaks down into ammonia, which creates an unpleasant odor. The second stage of decay produces mercaptans, which cause the most-serious odor problems. Mercaptans are the chemicals that give skunk spray and rotten cabbage their distinctive odors. Timing is vital. The sooner you eradicate both the stain and odor, the better.

Vinyl, tile, linoleum, and floors with similar surfaces are easy to clean. Simply soak up the puddle with paper towels or pick up the feces, then mop the floor with a sudsy cleaner, rinse, and follow with a nontoxic deodorizer, then let dry. Accidents on the carpet are a more serious matter and should be cleaned *immediately*. When ignored or undetected, urine can sink into the padding or the floor, and these stains are much more difficult—if not impossible—to remove. The best way to handle urine accidents on a carpet is to cover the spot with paper towels and stand on them, so that the paper towels absorb as much of the liquid as possible. Wet the stain with water or club soda, then blot with dry paper towels until all the moisture is again absorbed. Follow with a specialized urine-stain-and-odor remover. If the staining is severe, or you are concerned about damage, consult a professional carpet cleaner.

Cleaning the carpet with just water, club soda, household cleaners, or ordinary carpet cleaners will only mask the smell for a few days (never use ammonia-based products, because they smell like urine and will only encourage your dog to return to the same spot). You need an enzymatic cleaner that chemically dissolves urine and feces, so that your carpet no longer smells like a bathroom. There are many different kinds of nontoxic pet stain/odor removers for floors and carpets—Nilodor, Nilotex, Simple Solution Stain and Odor Remover, Nature's Miracle Two-Step Stain and Odor Clean-up, Get Serious Pet Stain Remover, Spot Not, No Scents, and House Saver, to name a few. Such products are not perfumed cover-ups; used according to directions, they instantly destroy the odor so the dog can no longer smell it.

If you smell an odor but cannot find the stain, try using a black light that causes urine to glow when all other lights are turned off. These can be purchased at Home Depot and Wal-Mart, or by mail or online from the pet-supplies catalogs listed at the end of this book.

As soon as your dog is trained to relieve himself outdoors, it is also your responsibility to clean up after him. Clean surroundings are essential for your dog's health. If the dog uses a toilet area in your backyard, train him to go to the same place each time so it can be easily cleaned or hosed down. Remove his feces promptly and dispose of them, especially if he makes a mistake on the sidewalk or on someone else's lawn. Many cities have scoop laws under which pet owners can be fined for not picking up after their dogs. Piles of animal feces are not only obnoxious-looking and -smelling, but can also produce disease. They (and the soil under them) can be infested with many types of canine worm larvae that, depending on the type, can stay alive for a short time in any outside environment. Healthy dogs can become infected when they eat feces or soil contaminated with worm larvae from other dogs. A dog can even get eggs on his nose just from sniffing infected feces and can become infected if he licks them off and swallows them.

A responsible pet owner is always considerate and picks up after his dog. You can buy various "pooper-scoopers" from your pet-supplies dealer. But if you can't picture yourself carrying such an uncouth-looking device, simply tuck a few small opaque bags in your pocket each time you take the dog out for a walk. After your dog defecates, pull out a bag, slip it over your hand inside out, and scoop up the feces. Pull off the bag by the open end and deposit it in the nearest trash receptacle.

HOUSEBREAKING AND
PAPER-TRAINING PROBLEMS

There are many reasons why dogs may refuse to become housebroken or paper-trained or why they may experience relapses in training. Whatever the problem, *correct it immediately and positively*. Ignoring stubbornness or regression is asking for trouble. You must act quickly to prevent any mistake from developing into a fixed pattern. Remember that a little patience and understanding can work wonders. Dogs are highly intelligent animals that respond enthusiastically to the right kind of corrective training.

Health Problems

The 7-day formula is based on your puppy's being in excellent health. Illness will delay or upset the training program. Indeed, never start the training program if your dog is ill. Kidney or bladder infections may make retention of urine difficult and painful. Worms and intestinal disorders can cause loose or bloody stools. It's difficult to housebreak a puppy that has no control over his bowel movements. Do remember that your dog cannot control runny bowel movements any better than you can. A fecal exam will determine whether the dog has worms or intestinal parasites. If you start the training program and it is not working, or if you notice such symptoms as vomiting, changes in appetite or water intake, genital discharge, constipation, straining, frequent or bloody urination or defecation, or fever (over 102.5° F or 39° C), have your dog examined by a veterinarian as soon as possible.

Normal urine is amber-colored and clear. A dog's age influences the degree of odor of fresh urine. Perfect kidney function in young puppies filters out much of the waste; as dogs grow older, the odor becomes more intense as the kidneys filter less efficiently. Normal bowel movements should be well formed and brown in color (although some dietary ingredients may make them darker or lighter).

Emotional Problems

Housebreaking and paper-training problems can be emotional in origin. Troublesome situations often develop when dogs become bored, frustrated, anxious, or spiteful. The arrival of another pet, a new baby, or even a visitor can make a dog feel that his territory is being violated, and he may start relieving himself all over the house.

Canine/Feline Rivalry—There are several things to consider if you are planning to own more than one dog, or a cat and a dog (surprisingly, they can become closer companions than two dogs). Much depends on the temperament of the pet you choose and the emotional reactions of your present pet, but dog-and-dog and dog-and-cat can learn to coexist peacefully. With dogs, the adjustment should present fewer difficulties if the second is a member of the opposite sex. Although you may encounter a few petty quarrels, there is always less hostility between dogs of different sexes. If the two are not intended for breeding purposes, however, have them neutered/spayed as soon as they mature, in order to avoid unwanted pregnancies. There will be much less aggravation between two dogs of the same sex if they, too, are neutered/spayed. If you must have two dogs of the same sex, life will be less aggravating if the second dog is a puppy. Adult dogs are usually more hospitable to a puppy or a kitten than they are to a full-grown dog or cat.

A little common sense will get you through the adjustment pe-

riod. If the new arrival gets all the attention, the first dog will probably feel threatened. Therefore, the first dog should be loved and
fussed over before anything else. Once he learns he's still cherished
by the family, you can start paying attention to the newcomer without hurting the first dog's feelings. Each dog needs a "den" of his
own, and each should have separate feeding dishes spaced far
enough apart to avoid fights over food. Until you're sure that the two
animals get along, keep them separated when they are unsuper-
vised. It should only take a short time for both pets to settle into a
regular routine.

A New Baby in the Family—A new baby can cause severe emotional trauma, especially to a dog that has considered himself the
family's "only child." If your dog is not used to children, ask some

friends with youngsters to come to your house. Observing the interactions between the dog and the children can give you an inkling of how he might behave in the future. If your dog is not easy to control and you haven't already done so, now is a good time to begin an obedience-training program before the baby is due. The mother-to-be should take part in the training if she can, because it's likely she will be alone much of the time with the dog and the baby. And when she is feeding, holding, or carrying the baby, being able to make the dog sit, stay, or lie down with voice commands could be crucial. Obedience training will be helpful, too, when the baby begins to crawl and to throw his or her toys on the floor.

Expect your dog to be very inquisitive when you bring the baby home. Introduce the two gradually, but don't ever leave the dog alone with the baby. Lead the dog to the crib or bassinet and let him look while you praise him lavishly and stroke him. Don't be disturbed if he regresses and starts acting like a puppy. Many a well-mannered dog has been known to "brand" a carpet or two after the appearance of a new baby.

If the dog misbehaves in any way, confine him to his den when you can't look after him. Don't suddenly ignore him, or he'll be very confused. Cooping him up while everyone rejoices over the baby will only make the dog more jealous. Lavish as much attention and affection as possible on the dog. It should take only a short time for him to settle down.

If your dog does not learn to accept your baby eventually, however, consult a professional trainer or, if the dog seems belligerent, consider finding him a new home.

Separation Anxiety—Anxiety may make some dogs relieve themselves indoors. They become indignant when they are separated from their owners for long periods and deliberately urinate and defecate indoors even after they have been housebroken. Confining a dog to a small den—his crate, or behind an adjustable pet gate—when you are out is the only solution. Don't pay attention to your dog for at least 30 minutes before you go out. Be sure to provide the dog with his favorite toys or chew bones. When you return home, do not greet or fuss over your dog; instead, wait until he settles down and becomes more laid-back.

Dogs, like children, can also develop behavioral and emotional problems as a result of family tensions and clashes. Each time you raise your voice to another family member or to a friend, your dog can become so upset that he will urinate and defecate indoors to relieve *his* tensions.

Habitual Spot Staining

Friends of mine had a Maltese named Brutus that took great pleasure in letting loose on a particular spot on the living-room carpet. They blotted, and they cleaned, and they disinfected, but to no avail. Brutus kept returning to the same spot to deposit his puddles and plop-plops. Things looked bad for Brutus until his owners decided to try the spot-feeding program as a last resort. It solved the problem and Brutus and his owners lived together happily ever after.

If your dog, like Brutus, repeatedly urinates or defecates in a certain area of your house, remember the den-dweller's reluctance to eliminate where he eats, and the solution to the problem becomes very simple: *feed your dog at that very spot.* Be sure to thoroughly clean and deodorize any soiled area, then leave the food dish down between meals to discourage the dog from returning to resoil it. Continue the spot-feeding program for at least seven days, and then resume feeding at the dog's regular place. Should the dog have a relapse, use the spot-training again until the problem is solved. Don't give up. It sometimes takes as long as six weeks to break older dogs of this habit. (The spot-feeding program can be used to solve urine and spraying problems with cats, too.) If you own more than one dog and have trouble determining which one is defecating in the house or off his paper, drop a little green or red food coloring in one dog's food. The color will show up in the dog's stool, and the culprit will be quickly identified.

"Dribbling," or Submissive Urination

Some puppies or older dogs may pass a little urine when you bend down to pet them, when you discipline them, when you talk in a loud voice, when you arrive home after an absence, or when friends come to visit. The pet may dribble urine while he is standing, or he may roll over on his back and urinate while exposing his genitals to you.

Such behavior is not related to housebreaking problems but rather to over-submissiveness. Dribbling is one of the signs of submissive behavior, and subordinate dogs often do this to dominant dogs and to people. The dog does not know he is urinating; the act is an involuntary reflex. Scolding, spanking, rubbing his nose in urine, and other negative forms of punishment, therefore, will not solve the problem. The solution is to raise your dog's confidence level and to avoid actions that trigger submissive urination:

- Do not bend over to pet or to greet your dog if it causes him to urinate. Crouch down instead, making your body appear less aggressive.

- Avoid placing your hand on the dog's head. Instead, with your palm upward, pet under the dog's chin or on the throat. It's much less threatening than putting a hand on his head.

- Use the phrase "Good dog!" while you are petting, and also when you put down your dog's feeding dish. Each time your dog does something right, praise him lavishly and say "Good dog!"

- When you return home after an absence, don't greet your dog immediately and *don't make eye contact with him*. Eye contact, which is associated with dominant behavior, can intimidate a submissive dog and make him urinate. Look above your dog's head at first. Don't fuss over the dog for at least 5 minutes, even if he's wildly jumping up and down. When you finally do approach the dog, crouch down instead of bending over.

- Arriving guests should be advised not to greet your dog but to sit down immediately and ignore him. If the dog approaches them, they may talk to him softly, but without making eye contact. Under no circumstances should they approach the dog.

- Avoid all reprimands and harsh tones of voice, particularly if these have caused urination in the past.

- Obedience training will help build your dog's confidence and give him a greater sense of security. Experienced instructors throughout the United

States offer private lessons (where dog and owner
train at the trainer's school or in the owner's home)
and group classes. You can find them in the yellow
pages under "Pet and Dog Training." Also, local
kennel clubs, obedience-training clubs, humane and
civic organizations, and 4-H clubs often sponsor
group classes, which are usually held in some public
facility. Owner and dog attend class for an hour each
week, then reinforce the training by practicing at
home every day.

Follow these suggestions faithfully and you should notice a
change within a short time. The problem should be corrected within
four to six weeks.

Indoor Urine Marking: The Persistent Leg Lifter

A very serious problem involves the male dog that lifts his leg to
urinate all over your furniture and walls. Leg lifting is not a housebreaking problem, but rather a behavioral problem. Chronic leg
lifters are urine-marking to establish their territories. They may be
jealous of a new baby, another pet, or a visitor in the house, or they
may be emotionally stressed and want to prove their supremacy.
They are really expressing their dominance as a "pack member."

Dogs mark territory, vertical objects, and occasionally, other animals or people by lifting their legs and urinating (they rarely mark
with feces). When a dog is "marking," the quantity of urine is small,
in contrast to the larger amount usually discharged when he is truly
relieving himself. Some females also mark; they do it from a squat-
ting position. Urine marking is more common in unneutered males
and females, but it does occur in a small percentage of neutered

dogs. Marking, according to veterinarians, may start as early as twelve weeks of age and generally increases recurrently until the dog is two or three years old.

Outdoor territory marking is a normal part of a dog's pack-member behavior. It is a "calling card," announcing the dog's presence to other dogs in the area and, in turn, informing that dog which strange animals are in the vicinity and how recently they passed by. In the wild, the size of a dog's territory generally indicates his degree of dominance. A dominant dog will mark as large a territory as possible, while a more submissive animal may urinate in one small area if that is all the space he can confidently defend. Persistent indoor urine marking can be corrected in some cases by giving the dog confined in a house the opportunity to exercise and mark his territory outdoors.

Reprimands and punishment will not solve this problem. Marking behavior stems from the male hormone testosterone (females also produce small quantities) in intact males. Unless you plan to breed your dog, the most sensible solution to indoor urine marking issues is to have the dog neutered (that is, a male castrated or a female spayed). According to Dr. Nicholas Dodman of Tufts University, "approximately 60 percent of unaltered male dogs will cease urine marking within weeks or months of castration, and estrus-related urine marking will be abolished in virtually all females once they are spayed." Neutering also makes a male dog less likely to want to roam, less aggressive, and a more even-tempered pet. Unspayed females tend to develop uterine infections and ovarian and mammary tumors as they age. Spaying will prevent these problems later in life.

The best time to neuter or spay is when a dog is about six months old, before he or she becomes sexually mature. The operation can be performed at any age, but the longer you postpone it, the more likely the marking behavior may become an established habit that is more difficult to break.

Even if you think your dog will not mark while you are in the house, keep him under close surveillance at all times. If you see him begin to urinate inside, distract him with a loud sound (an empty soda can into which a few pennies have been dropped makes a good noisemaker), grab him by the collar or pick him up, and take him outside. Praise him lavishly when he urinates outside. If you are unable to watch the dog, confine him in his den and take him out faithfully at the times indicated on the housebreaking schedule. Another solution is to put him on a leash and tether him to you in the house for a few days. Use a 6-foot or 12-foot training leash, depending on the size of your dog. Tie the handle around your wrist or loop it onto your belt; you'll always know what your dog is doing and where he's going. Confine the dog every time you go out.

This also is a good time to begin obedience training; it will help you establish a good rapport between you and your dog and make you a more consistent pack leader. You will be able to control your dog's actions by teaching him such basic commands as "Come," "Heel," "Sit," "Stay," and "Down."

Don't forget to thoroughly clean and remove all traces of urine odor from furniture, carpets, and drapes, so the dog won't be tempted to return to those spots and mark them again. Try the cleaning and deodorizing hints found on pages 61 and 62 first; however, the accumulated odors from months of previous marking will probably require the services of a professional home-furnishings cleaner.

If these suggestions fail, talk to your veterinarian about medication therapy as a last resort. Certain antidepressant and antianxiety medications help to reduce territorial marking in uncastrated males.

Country Dog/City Dog

A new home can produce housebreaking lapses. Moving from the city to suburbia or to the country means that your dog probably will urinate and defecate on grass rather than on pavement. That's not as difficult a change as transplanting a country dog to a city, but in either case, you must establish a precise walking schedule and take your dog out *on time* and praise him lavishly when he relieves himself.

Dog ownership in the city is a great responsibility. You may think urban life is stimulating, but it can be traumatic for a dog, with constant noise, excessive traffic, horns blowing, crowds of people, elevators, and hard pavement. Dogs that live in apartment houses have to learn to control the call of nature not only in their lodgings but also in the halls, elevators, and the lobby. If you can carry your dog outside for the first few days of the training period, it will help reinforce the fact that he has to hold things until he reaches the curb.

Often, retraining a country dog to use the city streets takes weeks of untiring patience. The toughest housebreaking problem my husband and I ever faced was when we moved from the suburbs to downtown Manhattan. All our dogs adjusted quickly to city life, except for Plum, a five-year-old Whippet. Although she was leash-trained as a baby, Plum never needed to be led outside and always did her duty running free in our backyard, a quiet and enclosed acre of ground. Suddenly her freedom and tranquility were gone, and she was forced to urinate not only on leash, but also on pavement, and in the midst of noisy New York City. Hounds are known to be rather single-minded, and, true to her heritage, Plum resisted the change for weeks. She was so unyielding that we thought she would burst from retention. She even regressed and decided that our living-room shag rug was a far better toilet area than the turbulent street. It took several weeks of consistent scheduling, patience, and many long walks to achieve success. And when she did her duty outside, we really smothered her with praise. We took her everywhere—to stores and sidewalk restaurants—to condition her to the noise and crowds of people, too. The key phrase is *don't give up!* Plum eventually became the most cosmopolitan of dogs: she fancied riding in taxicabs, getting treats from the French bakery in our building, and loved being the center of attention at Bloomingdale's.

IN CONCLUSION...

If, as advised in the Introduction, you have read this book from beginning to end before undertaking any of the procedures, you should understand the concept of the training program. "But it's too hard-hearted," you say, "I couldn't put my puppy in a cage or confine him to the bathroom or kitchen."

Nonsense! I've trained many dogs using this method, and they are all happy, well adjusted, and *housebroken*. The basic program takes only seven days, depending on the dog's age. Try it and you'll see that once everything falls into place, it makes sense and it works. Once your trained puppy becomes an adult, he'll need to relieve himself less frequently and his outdoor or papering schedule will seldom vary. The same is true for older, previously untrained dogs, and dogs that were once housebroken but have regressed.

Here are some basic rules to remember:

1. Dogs are easy to train because they are pack animals with strong instincts to follow a leader. Learn to understand your dog's inherited behavioral instincts and work with, not against, them.

2. Don't expect to *completely* housebreak, paper-train or litter pan train a puppy under sixteen weeks of age, because he does not have full muscle control. Very

young puppies can't hold bladder and bowel
movements for long periods.

3. Decide what form of training—outdoor
   (housebreaking) or indoor (paper- or litter pan)—
   fits your lifestyle. Once the decision is made,
   consistency from your entire family will expedite the
   training program and make your dog a better-
   adjusted pet.

4. Feed your dog a nutritious diet on a consistent
   schedule and he will eliminate on a consistent
   schedule.

5. Do *not* feed him doggie treats or table scraps between
   meals during the training program.

6. Until your dog is housebroken, paper- or litter pan
   trained, the best way to teach him to control his body

functions is to create a "den" and confine him to it until it's time to go outside or to have a free period. Supervise your puppy at all times when he is out of his den.

7. Select one corner of a room (for the paper or litter pan) or one location outdoors (for housebreaking) as his toilet area. Consistently using one location makes cleanup easier. Additionally, the "scent" that remains at this location will encourage your dog to "go" when you lead him there.

8. During training, take your dog to his toilet first thing every morning, after every meal or drink of water, after naps, after play periods or excitement, and before bedtime.

9. In between, stay alert for signs such as whining, acting restless, sniffing the floor, or going around in circles. As soon as you see him doing these things, rush him to his toilet area.

10. Praise your dog lavishly every time he relieves himself in the correct place.

11. Use praise, not food, as a reward for housebreaking.

12. Clean up promptly after your dog.

13. Never physically punish your dog for his mistakes. The words "No" and "Bad dog" are the only corrections you need.

14. Always keep your dog clean and well groomed.

15. Follow a strict timetable. The more vigilant you are in the beginning, the more successful the training program will be. If your dog is not completely trained at the end of the 7-day period, the major part of your work will still have been completed. Just stick to the schedule a little longer. You'll be rewarded with a happy, obedient, and trustworthy animal.

WHERE TO BUY A CRATE OR
CAGE AND OTHER SUPPLIES

Dog crates and cages come in a variety of sizes to accommodate extra-small, small, medium, medium-large, large, and giant-sized breeds. Some are fold-down designs with carrying handles that make them ideal for travel. Remember: buy one made of 6- and 9-gauge or 7- and 11-gauge sturdy, closely spaced wire (the lower the gauge, the tougher the wire) with a "dog-proof" latch. Most pet stores, especially Petsmart and Petco, plus megastores such as Wal-Mart and Target, stock a complete selection of crates, cages, portable exercise pens, puppy "Piddle Pads," and products for stain and odor control. You can also order by mail or online. The companies listed below will send you an illustrated catalog on request, or you can browse online. All accept major credit cards.

PetEdge
P.O. Box 128
Topsfield, MA 01983-0228
1-800-738-3343
www.PetEdge.com

Doctors Foster & Smith
2253 Air Park Road, P.O. Box 100
Rhinelander, WI 54501-0100
1-800-826-7206
www.DrsFosterSmith.com

The Dog's Outfitter
Humboldt Industrial Park
1 Maplewood Drive
Hazelton, PA 18202-9798
1-800-367-3647
www.dogsoutfitter.com

RECOMMENDED READING
AND VIEWING

BOOKS

Baer, Nancy, and Steve Duno. *Leader of the Pack*. New York: HarperInformation, 1996.

Campbell, William E. *Behavior Problems in Dogs*, 3rd ed. Grants Pass, OR: BehavioRx Systems, 1998.

Dodman, Nicholas. *Dogs Behaving Badly: An A-to-Z Guide to Understanding and Curing Behavioral Problems in Dogs*. New York: Bantam Books, 2000.

Fox, Michael W. *Understanding Your Dog: Everything You Want to Know About Your Dog but Haven't Been Able to Ask Him*. New York: St. Martin's Press, 1992.

Kilcommons, Brian, and Sarah Wilson. *Good Owners, Great Dogs*. New York: Warner Books, 1999.

Lachman, Larry, and Frank Mickadent. *Dogs on the Couch: Behavior for Training and Caring for Your Dog*. New York: Overlook Press, 2001.

Monks of New Skete. *How to Be Your Dog's Best Friend: The Classic Manual for Dogs*, revised and updated ed. New York: Little, Brown, 2002.

Siegal, Mordecai, and Matthew Margolis. *Solutions: For Your Dog and You*. New York: Simon & Schuster, 2001.

Thomas, Elizabeth Marshall. *The Social Lives of Dogs: The Grace of Canine Company*. New York: Simon & Schuster, 2000.

Tiz, Joy. *I Love My Dog But . . . : The Ultimate Guide to Managing Your Dog's Misbehavior*. New York: HarperCollins, 1999.

Wood, Deborah. *Help for Your Shy Dog.* New York: John Wiley & Sons, 1999.

WEBSITES

The Internet can be a valuable source of information about housebreaking and its problems, as well as learning more about dog behavior, illness, and wellness in general. Some excellent sites to consult are:

- **www.petplace.com** (Backed by Massachusetts SPCA Angell Memorial Animal Hospital. First-rate information. My personal favorite.)
- **www.hsus.org** (Humane Society of the United States)
- **www.aspca.org** (American Society for the Prevention of Cruelty to Animals)
- **www.sspca.org** (Sacramento, California, SPCA)
- **www.dogpatch.org/obed/obpage2.cfm** (extensive training/behavior advice)

ABOUT THE AUTHOR

Shirlee Kalstone is an internationally recognized expert on pet care. She is the author of fourteen books about dog and cat breeds, pet health care, first aid, and grooming, plus countless articles in various magazines. She has lectured on pet care and grooming across the United States, Canada, and Europe, as well as in Argentina and Japan. Mrs. Kalstone was the founder and organizer (for eighteen years) of one of the largest pet health care/grooming conferences in the world. She and her husband have also bred and shown Poodles, Whippets, English Setters, Cocker Spaniels, Weimaraners, and Burmese and British Shorthair cats. Mrs. Kalstone lives in New York City.